CHARTING THE LOST CONTINENT

PRAISE FOR CHARTING THE LOST CONTINENT

"Linda Albert's poems resonate with the quest to be heard, the challenge to continue emerging, and the search for a meaningful life. Kudos for her exquisite words that plumb our emotions. As she so eloquently writes, 'It isn't always easy-this struggle, this so-called journey into wholeness.'"

—Nancy K. Schlossberg, Ph.D., author of *Too Young to be Old* and other books on transitions and aging
www.transitionsthroughlife.com

"*Charting the Lost Continent* is a celebration of womanhood. Linda Albert is truly a master poet. Over the years, I have read her poems one-at-a-time, and have always been profoundly moved by her poetic vision into and about the many dimensions of womanhood.

"Linda's poetry brings to mind the image of a rhizome. Always hidden under the surface of the earth, it sends its roots deep into Mother Earth, and, above ground, it sends up stems with its fruits into the light of day. Through the lens of her own life, her own rhizome, Linda's poems reveal the deep roots, and complex fruits of womanhood—our moods, thoughts, joys, sorrows, and deepest yearnings.

"Through this volume of poems, Linda Albert has found that illusive Lost Continent, which so aptly symbolizes womanhood. Now, that I have read this volume of her collected poems, I see that she achieves what all poets hope to accomplish. Upon reading *Charting the Lost Continent*, I am held in that place, which James Joyce called a state of esthetic arrest—that moment when the reader finds herself in a state of awe, or "ah ha!" At this moment, I am held safely inside Linda's vision, her rhythms, and her word, and am filled with beauty, truth, magic, radiance, deep happiness, and satisfaction—and am given a new sense of myself as woman."

—Bonnie L. Damron, PhD, LCSW, Archetypal Pattern Analyst
www.drbonniedamron.com

"Her preface poem declares that the reclaiming and charting of The Feminine requires 'heart and steel.' Linda Albert lives and writes with both those qualities. In a long career as an educator and consultant, she has been her own best healer, and describes a peak healing moment as 'a jolt in every cell.' In this collection of powerful poetry, Linda nourishes the reader with the 'stew' of herself, so she 'won't / have to die / uneaten.' She shares with us her dreams, her wisdom, her dark humor in generous ways that make them part of our own rich stew. She's willing to be our compassionate witness 'when it's your turn' at *Four A.M.* From the mysterious (but recognizable) 'This' in the poem *Untitled*, to the delightful (and recognizable) lure of the fridge in *Lorelei*, this collection is a pathfinder and welcome companion for the reader's (extra)ordinary life."

—Cynthia Trenshaw, MTh, author of *Meeting in the Margins: An Invitation to Encounter Society's Invisible People*, and *Mortal Beings: poetry*

"This book of poetry brings us into a sacred domain, opening vistas and truths in a voice we can all too easily understand. One does not so much read these words, but listens to the stories of a wise one, teaching us about life, transgressions, benevolence and ultimately reflecting on the ending of life.

"The poet's words linger as a refrain from a haunting melody, making us smile, remember, tear up, recalling the miracle of our children's birth, while knowing that our time is nearly over. Each refrain draws us into a story about life, about thresholds we have had to cross. 'Welcome back, Welcome back,' and we are brought to our knees remembering those times when a warm smile erased our fears of being cast off. Then, without asking, she reminds us that 'flesh and spirit must take separate bows,' while admitting to being, 'afraid to go where I have never been.' Linda Albert's words are wings carrying me to places I need to go."

—Michael Conforti, Ph.D.Director, Assisi Institute, Jungian analyst, author, lecturer, and film script consultant

"Linda Albert takes us on a journey through the internal world of inquiry while intertwining mythology with the details of daily life and aging.

She leads us through Persephone's underworld up through the creative source, 'Those creative juices—like the red grapes/ in the glass dish on the top shelf/ of the refrigerator, now wrinkled as raisins.'

"Albert takes us from the deepest human yearnings and regrets to the 'joys of peanut butter' and 'a wooden desk lit by a window.' With naked awareness she illustrates the landscape of life and its betrayals: 'If I could, I would tear this betrayal off/ like sagging nylons.' As she charts this lost continent, we are brought home to ourselves and she tells herself '…refuse to suffer over suffering.' Focusing on the feminine, her poetry includes all—Jung's anima and animus."

—Clara Rosemarda, author of *Doing Laundry*, *Naked Branches*, and *Steeped: In the World of Tea*

"Poems filled with feminine strength and power. A deep dive into the secret spaces in Everywoman's heart."

—Carol Gino, RN, MA, *New York Times* bestselling author of *The Nurses Story* and *Me and Mario: Love, Power & Writing with Mario Puzo, Author of the Godfather* www.carolgino.com

"Through her honest portrayal of the lived experience, Linda Albert's poetry brings to the reader the knowing smile of recognition. In *A Question of Time* she posits that 'sometimes all the pieces do come together and there is time to tell the whole story.' Her poetry is a collection of many stories providing insight and humor, the sweet and the bittersweet, powerful and poignant observations on life and living. In *When They Were Born* she writes, 'These days no rituals exist for adults to go alone into the wilderness of their own lives, face demons and catastrophes from which no one else can save them.' If not the ritual, Albert's poetry provides the beauty, the solace and the magic to at least make meaning of the journey."

— Anne E. Mulder, PhD., retired Community College President, University Dean and Professor of Higher Education

"The poems in Linda Albert's *Charting the Lost Continent* are well crafted and filled with wisdom and sensual insight. There is 'still time, though late, to bloom another season, to write the story,' she tells us, for 'the dead leave their auras behind for us to carry.' Linda's authentic and brave revelations are a map for her readers to use as a guide through loss and growth into praise song."

—Linda Leedy Schneider, LMSW, psychotherapist in private
practice, writing and poetry mentor, workshop leader for
The International Women's Writing Guild, and author of
Some Days: Poetry of a Psychotherapist

"In poetry, Linda Albert seemingly allows herself to experience life unmasked and unshielded from the intensity of her own inner truth. And, in reading and soaking into her poignant metaphors, my own mask dissolves long enough for a quick unshielded glimpse at my own inner truth."

—D. Beth Macy, Ph.D. Organizational Development and
Bohmian Dialogue consultant, author and practitioner

"Linda Albert, poet/sorcerer, unspools fearless verse into the achingly intimate territory of the elegiac, plumbs the unanswerable, then flares her cape to reveal an *Ode to a Peanut* and a glimpse of her *Moon Garden*. I hear a cello."

—Lucia Blinn, author of *Sonoma, Memo to Marty*, and
We Can't Live in Queens

"With rapier wit and humble heart, Linda explores the seasons of life, distilling her 82 years into poems with soul and humor. She expertly weaves together mythology, feminism and fairy tales, dressing herself in the bones of daughter, mother, wife, grandmother, poet, lover, thinker. From diapers to death, Linda is fierce, honing the poet's knife to cut through and into the reality of what makes a life. She spares us nothing but the truth lived through the fire of meticulous thought and iambic pentameter. She has set a rich feast before us, with amuse-bouches, tempting morsels, deeply satisfying dishes, rich desserts. May her book feed your soul as it has mine."

—Silvia Behrend, D. Min, M. Div, Certified Pattern Analyst,
Educator, Mentor, Senior Faculty at the Assisi Institute,
www.behrendcounseling.com

"Poetry, if well done, offers us a threshold into that world where deep calls unto deep, and we are connected with an archetypal reality that speaks with a thousand voices. In this book, Linda Albert ushers us across that threshold and brings us into an intimately nuanced world of feminine psyche and soul. She has woven a verbal tapestry of such eloquent honesty and courageous vulnerability it had me wiping tears and shouting, Yes! This!"

—Loralee M. Scott, MFA, Founder and Director,
Seeing Red www.seeingredconference.com

"This collection of poems takes Linda Albert's readers on a courageous journey of navigation and discovery within the familiar worlds of family, personal loss and gain, lessons learned, and hopes for resolution. Hers is a voice of wisdom, often calling upon myth to illustrate the timeless qualities of human experience, yet also grounded in contemporary life where being a woman and a poet are gifts that both gratify and challenge. Read *Charting the Lost Continent*, knowing you can follow Albert's map to find a way to love this fleeting life."

—Miriam Pederson, Emeritus Professor of English, Aquinas College
Author of *This Brief Light* and chapbooks of collaborative poetry
and sculpture

"Linda Albert's poetry gracefully reveals her contemplation of a life fully lived. She says—and clearly demonstrates through her writing—that she is '. . . still in the mental morning of life' while, at the same time, she exhibits the wisdom that comes with age, with living through the deaths of friends, with 'the blows life sends us.' I love the way she sums it all up in her poem *What Matters Now*. Her answer? The poem."

—Georgia Court, Owner, Bookstore1 Sarasota and Founder,
PoetryLife Festival

"Revealing, relatable, and provocative, the interior recesses of a fully-lived life are laid bare in Linda Albert's *Charting the Lost Continent*. Here the reader finds connection through a deeply moving examination of the human experience, womanhood, and the arc of one individual's life. This collection is a homecoming; a contemplative garden in which to linger."

—Lynne M. Burns, M.A.Ed., professional educator, storyteller, and student of Dr. Clarissa Pinkola Estés (author of *Women Who Run with the Wolves*)

"Linda Albert's poetry captures the life cycle of the heart's secret joys and griefs from birth through aging. Her keen observations of the routine to the sublime, prod us to re-examine our own search for (our authentic self,) meaning (and purpose) in the changing landscape of our lives. Like bite-sized meditations, these poems can be savored over and over again."

—Rachel Epstein, L.Ac., J.D.
Co-Author of *Reversing the Trauma of War: A PTSD Imagery Handbook for Veterans, Active-Duty Personnel, and Their Families*
Director, American Institute for Mental Imagery
www.drjerryepstein.org

CHARTING THE LOST CONTINENT

LINDA ALBERT

Poetry and Other Discoveries

Rainbow River Press, Biddeford Pool, Maine

Cover illustration by Noppharat - stock.adobe.com.
Book & cover design by Six Penny Graphics

Trade paperback ISBN: 978-0-9823991-5-6
Ebook ISBN: 978-0-9823991-6-3

For further information and permissions approval or to order copies of this book, go to www.LindaAlbert.net.

Library of Congress Control Number: 2019911917

Albert, Linda, 1937—
Charting the Lost Continent: Poetry and other discoveries / Linda Albert.
ISBN 978-0-9823991-5-6 (original trade pbk. : alk. Paper)—
ISBN: 978-0-9823991-6-3 (ebook)

First Edition, 2020

Printed in the United States of America

To my mother, Lucille Janet Lee,
who always wanted me to write a book,
and to the inner Divine who cast the deciding vote
on which book I should write—and when.

AUTHOR'S NOTE

Publishing this book at the age of 82 seems
both long overdue, yet perfectly timed.
I offer it to you with love.

—Linda Albert, 2020

Contents

I

II

III

IV

The Feminine flourished like Atlantis once
until, blamed for life and also death,
her suckling and such cruelty feared,
an ancient cataclysm swallowed her whole,
submerged her stories under the sea.
Fathoms deep, she slept for eons,
hinted at, but best forgotten.
Now, despite that, shelves of shale,
multitudes of mangrove roots, layered
limestone beaches thrust themselves upward
after long, chaotic labors. It is a difficult business
helping to birth a continent, crying out for skills of all
to make the new/old landmass whole and seamless—
heart and steel to chart it.

—The Author

|

Objects Closer Than They Appear

I'm lying on my side
curled in a spiral
like the shell my grandchildren
found at the beach,
happily reading—
an occupation more satisfying
than sex some days—when
I spy a limb wrinkled as old fruit,
or a sheet left too long in the dryer.
At first, I can't believe
this could possibly belong to me.
I contract my muscles to prove
mistaken identity, but see
it's my hand holding the book,
my hand with veins starting to look
like tributaries of rivers,
fingers growing arthritic knobs;
the skin on my arm pleats
like an accordion at certain angles.
If I could, I would tear this betrayal off;
throw it in the trash like sagging nylons;
put on a pair with fresh elastic.
I have seen how this happens
to others, how epidermis
stretches while structure melts;
how even exercise
doesn't hold collapse at bay.
But I am still in the mental morning

of life. I'm not ready to wear
this ancient suiting. Whose arm
is this anyway?

Prodigal Daughter

A man went to confession. He expected
anonymity but the booth with grillwork
was gone. Only a young priest he knew
in other guises was there to greet him.

The man hadn't been to church in years,
carried coins for penance, was ready
for a beating. The priest only looked at him
and smiled. "Welcome back," was what he said.

The man told the story to a woman who
had come to him for guidance. Long ago
she'd lost the thread that held her
to her roots. Ashamed at such a failure,
she, too, prepared for punishment. Not beating
but banishment was what she feared.

Instead, the unexpected kindness of his story
dropped inside her like a pebble, the words
set up a ripple, became a repetition, slipped
past corners, fell through layers, melted ice
once used as walls. *Welcome back, Welcome back,*

Welcome back, became a singing deep inside her,
as dormant yellow tulips pushed themselves
to life through hardened clay, and defiant
red geraniums blazed through winter's freeze,
indifferent to their destiny in summer.

Welcomed back to ground for holding, encircled
by the ancient snake who bites its tail—still time,
though late, to bloom another season,
freed to write the story she was born to tell.

What Matters Now?

What matters now.
The unmade bed I want to straighten;
excitement in my chest—creative leaping;
the way I'm wed to my computer,
the poems spilling over without rest.

What matters now.
The pages that I long to fill;
the shirts I said today I'd iron;
the polish chipping on my toes;

the need to light a waiting candle;
the time I've missed to meditate;
what matters now?

The poem.

Expectation

What we want at first
seems easy: the warm black earth
of bodies joining, the planting
of those hybrid seeds,
the sunny dreaming.
We do not see our desperation;
the way we might be watering
with contaminated love, might drown
those fragile shoots too soon.
We want our children
to join their roots to ours,
to bloom so wondrously
that all will marvel.
We are ashamed if there are weeds,
alert to keeping worms at bay.
We do not know the dark
side of our wanting,
the poison in the oleander;
how the blossoms that we long for
might be destined to grow
in different gardens.
Instead we focus on the prize
we think should be our due—
the pride of our creation
our rose of immortality.

Beginning

It's a common complaint
and hard to forgive—
how birth,
morning or midnight,
is never easy.
How hard it is
to be peeled ripe
from the womb's warm harbor
into a life of lights and confusion,
fed thin milk
doled by a stranger,
with no guarantee
that by drinking
we will rise to the top
like cream.

Gemini in a Mood

She sits in the beehive
Believes she mourns for no one

Runs razors through her forelocks
Licks jelly from the jar.

Her fingers are red pencils
Her eyes are wearing bottles

She is drawing tiger lilies
On her toes and underwear.

She is lonely, she is angry
She is sure she's singled out

She will make the others pay for this—
Demeter's at the fair.

Where is poor Persephone
When everyone is hiding?

Even Hades has absconded,
Not a single seed to spare.

She is angry, she is frightened,
she is ready to kick ass here

She will summon all her demons
Comb Medusa through her hair.

She will dress herself in poison
She will tear her clothes to rags

She will thrill to all destruction
She will form a group of hags.

She is lonely in her beehive
But she doesn't want to leave

For it suits her in this kingdom—
Nothing left to do but grieve.

Waukegan, 1943

We came in winter. Father
in the Navy, lieutenant,
junior grade.
Mother miserable.
Father scared.
Brother, age two
with screwdriver, busy
unscrewing door knobs from our
rented house. I had
whooping cough. Undiagnosed.

Last Memory

April's not the cruelest
month. That time
is autumn when winds
come blowing
from the north, play havoc
with an aging body.
When sunlight
doesn't matter. Bones
can't walk away.
When father
has no reason
to get up
and eat his dinner.

Before

Before the Age of Reason
only one Thought was around

us. Wise-eyed creature-
Mother, still part ooze

and talons keeping us
in balance. We, as children,

rode atop her earth-womb,
reached out to each other,

innocent and free to play,
feeding from her strong maternal

beak—her lushly feathered
focus, locked within her

curved embrace.
Before the need for reason

made us seize the thought
that formed us;

before we killed the mother
in order to grow up.

Reflection
—After W.H. Auden's "Musée des Beaux Arts"

I remember it vividly—
how I was taking my nightly bath;
lying naked and a little chilly in the tub,
not thinking about anything special,
or pondering a different problem
as Auden knew the Old Masters
understood. Only this time
it was the relief of suffering—a jolt
in every cell so great my body
leaped. It's a wonder
I wasn't electrocuted—
found floating face down;
bath oil sliding in greasy scales
down my lifeless back, just now
when knowing could make my life
begin. The usual irony. But no;
there's also magic in these tales.
The mirror I'd looked in all those years,
the *Mirror, Mirror on the wall*
that kept me snared and found me wanting,
whose tarnished silver
backed a bleak and murky surface
rejecting light, was nothing but an object;
mirrors don't really talk or have opinions.
Amazing that I never noticed.

Turns out its voice was in my head;
the power was mine to name the seeing,
not a jealous Queen's who'd kill for my reflection.

The Old Masters must have also known
this human position;
how something momentous can happen
while someone else is sleeping or having a haircut
or Icarus has not fallen after all
into the sea.

Bone on Bone

I turned my back on some of your skills
before I really learned them—bridge parties,
lemon tarts with whipped cream piped around the edges,
three-layered tea sandwiches without the crusts—
because of all the hours I judged you'd lost there,
the chaotic kitchen, the clean-ups that always fell to me.

I got rid of your impatience
right from the beginning—
the time keeper tyrant
who kept you running until
it seemed to me you missed your life.
In that, I might have gone too far,
and now I want some back.

Your maxims, I weeded out along the way—
though I confess that job took years.
If it's true that God will only help the ones
who help themselves, then who needs God?
Airing dirty laundry in public is sometimes therapeutic.
The bed I make is not the one I always have to lie in;
There is no actual law.

But I do cherish your English bone china,
that set of thirty two with the gold rim and green border
you bought from Uncle Jack's jewelry store in Ottawa
and confirmed at the Sweet Sixteen
luncheon you made for me.

In fact, I think it would please you to know
I use that china every day.
Whenever I take a plate from the cupboard
I share the meal with you. It's easier now
since you've become my guest.

Indian Wedding Journal 1: On the Ganges

They call her Mother;
worship waist-deep

in her thick brown body—
like soup my mother used to make—

cleanse themselves to praise her;
anchor soap-sculpted limbs

to adoration, fingers
steepled together in prayer.

Their faces remind me of the way
my father looked in his coffin,

with the extraneous finally erased,
carved by his ancestors' bones.

Everything is brown and soothing,
like old movie film—

water, buildings, people, steps,
the smoke from the cremation fires—

(twice, by mistake, I write 'creation')
pagoda-shaped temples;

everything made of stone.
We light candles, cast jasmine

petal blessings, click camera shutters
to prove our presence.

Returning, our boat flies with the current,
invisible to the devout,

here, where they have weight
and we have none.

Recipe

I want to learn
to cook myself
like stew—
the meat of me,
the blood red wine,
rare mushrooms
hidden in the woods
of me, my secret
onion parts—deep earth
roots—potato-plain
and sweetly carrot,
the herbs, the salt
and pepper spice,
my tomato-self,
both tang and acid.

Simmer long and slow
in the big black enamel
roaster of souls until
I blend together, meld,
produce a richness,
flavor, texture,
a genuine bouquet.

Enough time covered
tightly in the dark
to heat clear through
before I have to boil

and bubble, pretend
to be a dish for serving.

Trusting the cook,
the stove, the process;
no longer a machine,
but food,
so life can finally get
its fill, and I won't
have to die
uneaten.

High Achiever

In her perpetual-motion
Rube-Goldberg
machine-life,
she is always
doing-for-tomorrow,
putting off
this one-time-only
never-to-come-again
today.

The Time-Keeper-Tyrant legacy
her family taught,
the *Energizer Bunny*,
the wind-up toy
that doesn't stop
until it wears itself out,
drops over,
batteries dead…
finished…
all-washed-up
kaput…

forever.

April Sonnet

I looked in wonder at this April town
and knew, like me, she woke up in a mood,

and dressing daylight in a dull gray frown
she sat down on her frozen bed to brood.

She grumbled that she'd had a wretched night
and didn't have a decent thing to wear,

then throwing on the drabbest gown in sight,
she combed bare branches through her wind-raked hair.

She filled the air with echoes of my sighs,
unlovely and unloved she also wept.

And newborn buds just opening their eyes
curled tighter in their lonely beds and slept.

Let all the birds of melancholy sing.
Tomorrow will be time enough for spring.

Tsunami

She's trying to understand her life.
Where she fits into the scheme of things.

Whoever made *The Rules* did not
have her in mind. A woman.

A Jew. The mother of a gay child.
Not loyal enough. Not thin

enough. Not ordinary enough.
Not humble enough. Not

perfect enough. Too spoiled.
Too smart. Too greedy. She thought

she was entitled to be happy. She
wanted her place in the sun. Her

piece of the pie. She wanted
to fit in. Can you imagine the gall?

She's lived her life as *Hans
Brinker*, occupied with plugging up

the leaks of poison, pain, and imperfection.
Not enough hands; fingers sore

and weary; the dam of her defenses
wearing out; new leaks

springing up. Water flooding in
from everywhere.

Tulip Bulbs

—for Sara and with thanks to Emily Dickinson

She brought me tulip bulbs that fall,
    "Here," she said,
    "plant them," she said.
    "They'll bloom next spring, I promise."

I had been dancing in the woods
when it happened. The sky turned black

suddenly, just like that; turning the
reds and yellows lifeless. Frightened

I said I had to leave; the children
would be coming home from school.

In the dream, my daughter's note
was in the kitchen. It was a message
but I couldn't read the words.

I never meant to dance the poet's tune.
This 'standing death' was never
in my plans, you see.
    "Do it now," she said.
    "The frost is only part way down."
    "It's not too late to plant the bulbs, I promise."

The clay was worse than rock.
It bruised my hands to dig.

The bending hurt my back.
    "Nothing can grow in this," I said.

In winter we made candles; wrecking
my only double boiler to gain a salmon pink

that didn't match and wicks so short
they barely held the flame.

    "It isn't any use," I said.
    "Just hang on 'til spring," she said.
    *"You never know what might happen
    if you can just hang on."*

They started through the earth in April;
tough, green shoots, pushing the stubborn
clay aside as though the struggle
was actually worth the trouble.

She brought me tulip bulbs that fall.
    "Here," she said.
    "Plant them,"
    she said.

Dream

The shoreline's shrunk
where she once walked

thick walls enclose it.
Breezes never freshen here.

No bird sails on an updraft.
Heat dries up every breath.

People clog the sand.
The water is too tired to move.

She tries to leave. The walls
turn into mazes. She can't

retrace her steps. Outside
streets empty; landmarks

disappear. Dark strangers
pave the road she thinks leads home

with new black asphalt. A hint
of open ocean lies beyond.

You Came as Swift and Silent as a Fawn

You came as swift and silent as a fawn,
While I lay unsuspecting through the night;
And then I woke, as startled as the dawn
To find the world I'd known had turned to white.
It was as if you'd raised a healing hand,
And mended Nature's wounds and scars so well,
That in some way I could not understand
I, too, was caught within your healing spell.
I wonder, if I'd felt a warning chill
In time to light the fire and lock the doors,
Would I be safe inside and sleeping still,
Or would I run out barefoot to be yours?

If I had known you'd come, but not to stay,
Could I have shut my eyes and turned away?

In the Land of the Goddess Where Nothing is the Way It Seems

It isn't always easy—this struggle,
this so-called journey into wholeness.

Who knows what voice is really speaking…
the Self, or is it Sloth that causes her

to sit with her husband's cast-off maroon
cashmere cardigan over her nightgown,

the space heater clicking a monotone,
an afghan over her knees, like an old lady

in a nursing home or a patient recovering
from awful illness. No drive to go anywhere,

all ideas gone. Is this the call to *home*
she reads about these days in books

by Jungian women authors, or is this fear—
the enemy she's run from all her life?

This is her dilemma—how to know the difference,
make peace with energy—sit

when it becomes a quiet pool, move
when it is moving. Hard to arrange a life that way.

What if it is stagnant water, not still at all, but brackish,
and she's a fool, the last to know?

She will drown here, die here, a nobody,
a do-nothing forever. Is this Hamlet or Ophelia

plucking mental daisy petals?
Can one do, and also be?

Life is hers to make or break,
a secret kept when she was young.

Few outer landmarks left to lead her,
now she is lost and also found.

She hopes the Soul is guiding.
The old map only went so far.

She is drawing this one as she goes along,
by hand, the only way she can.

First Thaw

Having just come through winter myself
I notice
sooty sentinels of snow
darkening the curbs,
crab apples pickled in sidewalk slush,
derelicts
of trash and twigs
sunk
in landlocked pools.

Streets are lined and pitted,
ancient faces
ruined before their time.
Sun whitens an albino sky;
its light reflects my ravage.

Only wind chime sounds of ice
melting
drop by drop by drop
from rooftops
and waterfalls singing into sewers
tell of something else to come.

Having just come through winter myself,
I listen.

Here Are the Sick Parts Coming up for Healing

Here are the sick parts coming up for healing:
See there, the tired one, the abused one,
the one whose head aches so.
See them shuffling:
the sad, despairing, hopeless one,
the angry one, the one nobody loves;
dragging, undernourished,
exhausted, like prisoners from Dachau.

She will not push them away,
medicate them, stuff them full of food
or work or entertainment, run from them,
lock them in the booby hatch;
poor suffering embryos of soul.

She will make them convalescent space
in the garden, in the backyard
where a mole has traced an underground river
in her grass; where buds are ready
to burst into bloom on every tree and bush;
where air is filled again with bird song.

She will feed them dry, toasted English muffins,
sun and sympathy to soothe their starved
and anxious stomachs; walk softly
so they won't be startled, bring them tea and afghans;
apologize for all the years she shamed them;

those long, unbroken years of winter
would have been enough to bear.

She will touch them gently;
their bones are thin and brittle.
Locked so long in cellars and in chains,
they can only take in tiny sips of love.
They are weak. They lie there
on lounge chairs on the patio.

All they can do
is breathe right now.
And even that is hard.

Responsible Party

My body, my hotel
has long been looking
for a home. No more
rented rooms in Hilton's
getting room service
of the spirit, or workshop-weary
Holiday Inns—now I'm looking
for a place to hang my stockings,
lay my head, a kitchen to feed
my soul that is mine. All
mine. A place I own, not
clean and decorate, reserve
for others.

In dreams these days
I am underdressed;
dancing naked in public
or wearing my nightgown
to funerals—lost, but trying
to find home. The coat
I hang in the hotel closet
is orange and isn't mine;
the funeral is elsewhere.

My body can't be measured
by the rented room any longer.
Now it's time to sign
a mortgage. Practice owning.
Call my body home.

At Taos Pueblo

Magenta morning,
Silver-haired Mother
makes fry bread,
weaves baskets,
forgives my earth hunger,
beans in belly,
tongue-happy taste.

Witch Dead, Spell Broken, Awakened Princess Connects with Pea

I'm having a love affair
with earth right now
all things brown, barren
rocky, earthy;

heart open womb wide
in the belly
something new grows
big it moves me.

Scared I want it
want it all want it now
want to die this way
body finally full.

This is the promise:
rock woos
earth heals
the Mother is forgiving.

Formal Viewpoint

—Again with thanks to Emily Dickinson

after a birth a formal viewpoint sometimes comes

Weathered bench:

Wood slats holding
butt and back,
head supported
by old adobe;
belly full.

Demeter has found her daughter again.

Trip to Hell
not so bad

in retrospect.

Sometimes

Like those first green shoots,
or that instant driving into dawn,

sometimes it happens, though rarely
when I'm expecting it of course,

those moments of connection so filled
with promise; so fresh, so fragile,

so fragrant, so possible…
that words are only shadows

and stillness is the proper anthem.
When all I can do is go on tiptoe

with arms opened and breath held,
watching and listening

for what awakens in the spaces
in-between.

The flower blooms. Day breaks.
Sometimes love happens.

If then, I'm quiet enough,
and present enough,

I can catch those moments
long enough to memorize them

and file away their promise
in the one sure place

I've learned
they can be found—

my own fresh, fragile,
possible human heart.

Ode to the Peanut

—For Jim

Let's sing a song of peanut butter,
The all-American spread.
That singular, savory, salubrious butter,
That symphony on bread.

Let's sing of the felicitous flavor that lingers
To the roof of the mouth or the licks of the fingers.

Sing of it smooth…

Sing of it crunchy…

For breakfast or dinner…

A meal or a munchy.

Sing of it piled on a crispy cracker;
Gourmet cuisine for the midnight snacker.
Sing of it plain…the manna of mannas;
Sing it with marshmallows, jam, or bananas.

Yes, let's all sing of peanut butter
And give three cheers and even a blessing.

And while you're all doing that, I'll go out to the kitchen
and make you a peanut butter, anchovy, and olive
sandwich with watercress, cucumbers, and French dressing.

Lorelei

I have a husband who doesn't quibble
With anything that's fit to nibble.
And anything he nibbles, he considers fit.
Even cold toast that the baby has bit.

When I've prepared a sumptuous dinner,
He doesn't label it a Pillsbury Winner,
Until he's sampled a generous smidge
Of leftover this or that from the fridge.

My husband has the remarkable knack
For turning a banquet into a snack.
He loves things canned, or frozen, or bottled;
Nor does he mind if they're minced or mottled.

My husband is a pleasure to cook for;
If you want to meet him just try to look for
A man who is simply and utterly unable
To get past the refrigerator to the dinner table.

Moon Garden

Plant me in a moon garden
Where I can thrive at night,
I whose moon is Cancer
Who comes alive at night.

Let me grow as *Evening Primrose,*
Lemon custard for my scent,
As I finish up my housework
In the quiet of the night.

Name me *Hesperis Matronalis,*
Purple Mother of the evening,
Dispensing aromatics
To my children in their baths.

Call my writing life Night Lily,
Maybe *Marvel of Peru,*
Who seeks jasmine scented metaphors
When ideas start to bloom.

Now I'm *Ipomea Alba*
Morning Glory of the night,
Fragrant and unfurling
As I listen to my heart.

I belong in a moon garden
At the end of a long day's tasks,
Where alone as *Angel's Trumpet*
I find vision, I find rest.

In Praise of PTA

At last for us has come to flower
That long awaited, wondrous hour!

No more the outcasts of the block;
The proud procession of the clock
Hast finally brought us to this day,
And membership in P.T.A.

We sallied forth like knights with sabers;
To march as one with all our neighbors
Be-ribboned and be-casseroled,
Protectors of one five-year-old.

With eagerness, and yet, forbearance,
We gathered with the *chosen* parents,
And offered up our steaming carton
In honor of the kindergarten.

At wee, small tables we dined, libated;
On chairs our offspring had vacated;
Mothers…fair, and fathers…strapping,
Seated proudly—(overlapping!)

No vineyard fruit could be more heady
Than one's first *P.T.A. Spaghetti*!

The Dog Years Are Upon Me

My children stick to me
the way *Jujubes* stick to your teeth.

Wherever I go, there is always a child
on top of me, behind, in front, or underneath.

And I find their fascination for me
absolutely extraordinary,

because as a constant companion
I am unquestionably ordinary.

Plus, it hasn't done me a bit of good
to have taken five courses in college psychology!

In fact, I wish I had been smart enough
to study toxicology,

since whenever I serve anything
other than hot dogs for dinner,

they act out a death by poison scene
that would put to shame an Oscar-winner.

Whereas they will willingly eat everything
but the Willow Ware when they go to visit granny;

Which is one thing I find not only traitorous
but uncanny.

Nor do I feel especially gracious or anything like
a goody-goody Samaritan

when they come home and turn right back
into hardcore *Hotdoggitarians.*

So you see, it's not the apron strings
of which I speak with so much blight and blustard,

it's simply that I have an itch
to cut the mustard.

When They Were Born

She watched as though
from another country,
the mirror positioned between
her legs, a more chaste picture
than she expected. She thought
she'd be humiliated by the exposure
but all she thought about
was her baby, struggling to get out
as each have had their struggles since,
while she—still thinking they were hers,
housed as they once were inside her—
taking her all to bring them to life—
and her job always to keep them there—
in life. "Stop pushing!" the doctor warned,
the cruelest words she'd ever heard,
when all her being was made for pushing.
"I can't," she croaked, but she obeyed;
Anything for those, her most creative gifts.

Now they are grown, as impossible
to believe as the original labors, and once again
she must stop pushing: "I didn't think I was,"
she says. "It's been so long since they left home."
But freedom comes at higher and higher prices,
both theirs and hers. These days no rituals exist
for adults to go alone into the wilderness of
their own lives, face demons and catastrophes
from which no one else can save them. No rituals

exist for mothers to let go, no midwives or
medicine men to cut belated cords.

Only fortitude and oxymorons can protect them
as they learn to share the distance
these second births demand.

Gender Negotiation

Once upon a time
I met a dragon. Instead of
getting into a power struggle
or fight, we sat down and
talked. (I'm not sure how
this happened. But it did.)
He said he felt unfairly treated,
poorly understood. He was a dragon
after all. He had to stay true to himself
didn't he? Fire-breathing
was in his nature. What could he do
about that? I told him I understood;
that he had every right to be his dragon self
but if he never let people know
he had feelings, was forever threatening
death by fire, he had to expect
there would always be opponents
out to slay him. He was so relieved
to tell his side of the story, he offered
to be my protector when I went
off into the unknown. I told him
it felt like protection enough
to finally understand him.

Sometime When the Oleander Bloom
—after William Stafford

Sometime when the oleander bloom, ask me
why I'm choosing to stay on this barrier island
when everyone else is fleeing. Ask me why,
when I've spent so much of my life staying safe,
I've joined you in making a home
where hurricane winds could destroy us.
Ask me whether this is love or insanity,
or why I'm not panicked at what a mistake
this could turn out to be.

I nod my head in surprise, and agree.
How pleasant it is when the car carriers and crowds depart
as we drive down this blossom-lined key
to own the oleander summer around us.
What a shame it would be not to feast in the blooming.
We know there is poison inside; hidden
winds and currents on the other side of the ocean
that could spell our disaster.

But everyone dies. That's what you tell me.
The news is not good anywhere.
This year it might be others who run to Samarra
while we and our few remaining neighbors
enjoy a reprieve; drink Chardonnay by the pool,
trade last minute stories, and ignore
our eventual fate.

A Small Bird Has Flown into My Chest

He flutters there;
trapped.
I swallow around twigs,
try to ignore the nest
mistakenly built
in my belly,
the planet's extra revolutions,
my limbs becoming lakes,
the helpless beaks,
the frozen sky.

My husband waits
for brain surgery
while all I can do
with my dizziness,
with the somersaults,
with the frantic bird,
is to hold as still as possible,
eyes fixed on the horizon
and pray not to fall.

Consider the Question Mark

How it curves around like cloak
or cutlass; protects or penetrates;
confusing, claustrophobic, yet
full of options; open for escape.

Consider the question mark:
the straight slide downward
ending in merry-go-round or whirlpool;
a place to drown or find adventure.

I live a life of questions:
Will we be spared the next hurricane?
Who will win the November elections?
Easier for this impatient soul.

Hard, the ones without end dates:
What to do with my life?
How to cope with all this pain and anger?
How long until my husband
cannot walk at all?

Last Straw

"Save me a bite of the brownie," I say as I hobble back into the foot doctor's office to see if someone can do something about the sharp fastener that is digging into my leg under the boot, now that I have graduated from soft cast to ACE bandage, which so far doesn't seem like much of an improvement. The nurse uses paper tape, but she doesn't seem thrilled to have to deal with me again.

When I get back to the car, mouth all ready for chocolate, tired from the heat and from always having to do the driving, even with my bum foot, the brownie is gone.

"You didn't save me anything?" I ask, unbelieving.

You think all the good things you do for someone else are without strings, but when that person can't even manage to save you a bite of a brownie, not even when you ask for it, not even one damned crumb, then goddamn, it is the last fucking straw.

"I told you to save me a bite," I shrill.

"What happened?"

"I was hungry," he says, looking straight ahead, not meeting my eyes.

I know you think I'm only talking about a brownie, for God's sake, and one bite at that. Not exactly what you'd think of as life or death. But it's been 20 years living with the challenge of his Parkinson's disease and that bite of brownie is a lot bigger deal than it sounds.

It's not every day a camel gets loaded up beyond its capacity to move. Go to Answers.com and see for yourself what happens when a "seemingly inconsequential addition" like a feather or single straw can lead to some kind of "cataclysmic failure."

Talk about the last straw. This camel's back is beyond broken. So is her sympathy. Or maybe it's her heart.

Of Physicists and Elegies

Nothing is ever lost...
so say the physicists. Matter transforms:
ice to water, water, air,
bulb, peony, mountain, cave,
mother, egg, boy, dust.
It doesn't help to know this.
My go-with-everything
black jacket, its silver snaps
celestial ash or unreturned
in some illicit closet. The patience I once had,
the firmer flesh of arm and thigh
transmuted badly—full to empty, hard to soft.

My college roommate, dead since April,
plays her fiddle where only angels
get to hear. The dopamine commands
that tell my husband's legs to move,
escape. His vocal cords cannot connect,
the whispered dial tone of his voice
a maddening wrong number.
I want them back the way they were.
The way they were, I want them.

I mourn for silver snaps, concertos,
husband, friend, flesh firm,
vociferous, ironic, moving—ironic flesh,
vociferous, firm and moving.

Four A.M.

When it's your turn
for the shit to hit the fan;
when it's your turn
for the health
of someone you love
to fall apart;
when it's your turn
to careen
from crisis to crisis
like dodgem cars
at the county fair;
when it's your turn
to live without sleep
and the food you eat
sticks in your throat
unchewed and untasted;
when it's your turn
for the space in your life
to be devoured
like the streets of Calcutta;
when it's your turn
to get too many phone calls
you don't have energy to answer
and too many flowers
you can't find time to water
and too many meals
that rot in your refrigerator
and the sick person

becomes a tyrant;
when it's your turn
to watch your children
turn into parents
trying to save what is

forever broken;

when it's your turn;
when it's your turn;
when it's   your   turn;

        it's
            your

                    t
                        u
                            r
                                n.

The Dream Changes at Midnight
—Upon Reading Amy Christman

But it's the same old dream:
I will lose 10 pounds,
become better organized,
clean my closets,
be more patient with my husband,
exercise regularly, floss every night,
get rid of clutter in my drawers.

The dream changes at midnight
but I don't change along with it.
I am the same old me,
carting myself along
like an old raincoat.
I can't start anew because
I don't have a new me to start with.

Every year it's the same thing.
Old mistakes make way for new ones.
Some grievances burrow deeper underground.
Most years, the clothes in the closets
just get squeezed more tightly;
the papers in the files bulge even more.
The seven pounds I lost last summer
must be lost all over. I still owe apologies
to someone somewhere.

There is no point claiming
the dream will change at midnight.
There are only so many seeds of willpower
on this planet. I simply have a share.
For every plot of land I've furrowed
there are others ready to go fallow.
How calming to discover
I can just dig in at midnight,
assured the new year
won't be all that changed
from last year, and all I need to harvest
is a good night's sleep.

This Is the Year the Dead Come Marching

This is the year the dead come marching,
not soldiers, accident victims,
strangers we cluck our tongues about
and then go back to eating, shopping,
making much of small things; no,
now it's a parade of people we know:
young, old, our age—the nerve—
old loves, old friends, the man who did our hair,
a new acquaintance full of promise,
a colleague, spouse, a child, a parent,
waving flags of their uniqueness in our faces,
leaving images of themselves—*Kirlian* photographs
implanted on our eyelids, their voices
engraved inside our ears.

This year, we're surprised by too many ghosts;
they deliver packages tumbled
with ribbons of memories confettied
with regrets. We're not ready for this.
There is unfinished business; forgiveness
we had yet to find, get well cards
we never got around to sending, soup
we never brought, words we thought
we still had time to say, caresses, hugs,
some needed thank-yous.

The dead celebrate their endings
despite us. The band is playing
just for them. They turn the corner
without us. They are at peace.
They leave their auras behind
for us to carry. The littered street
is ours to clean.

A Certain Joy

A certain joy has passed my way:
A certain joy has passed—
I knew, of course, it could not stay:
If joy, it could not last.

It was a momentary gift,
A tantalizing elf
Who gave my soul a sudden lift,
Then disappeared inside itself.

Go on and mock me, impish one!
I know your tricks; I'll play your game.
And pause beneath this winter sun
To weep because I've learned Your name.

Yes, I will chant a *mirologue*
For all the shifting grains of sand,
And when I'm done, if there's still fog,
I'll whistle 'til you find my hand.

A certain joy has passed my way.
A certain joy has passed.
I'd always known it could not stay.
If joy, it could not last.

It was a momentary gift,
That tantalizing elf

Who gave my soul a sudden lift
And left a memory of itself.

Who gave my soul a sudden lift
And left me larger than myself.

Unveiling
—The One Year Anniversary of his Death

Stillness under the olive tree
in Umbria at 7 a.m.
A well maiden
dug into prickly grass.
I imagine being filled
and then the emptying.
One lone tear at a time
trickles down my cheek
until I'm moved to hug myself.

We're here Jim, in Italy.
You gave me the world
and so I took it—scared
little girl lost these years
on top of the giant slide.
We came here together
to Umbria, to Rome
on a plane. Michael my
confessor, the Brooklyn angel
assured me it would be simple,
flying not with beeswax
but encased in metal, where
sitting my butt down on the seat
would be no different
than flying to Hartford,
only longer. The belief
that Michael would be

there to catch me
at the bottom of the slide.

The olives on the trees
wait for their ripening.
It's nice to feel free to sit still
under an olive tree in Umbria
in Umbria, in Umbria
without an agenda
a chance to sit and be.

Authentic Movement

I wanted the sun
the way a plant does.
Nothing I could do
would allow me to move
from the one spot I found it.
Planted to the ground
I stood, testing my limits
to see if I could move elsewhere
and still be happy,
feel warmed.
But only the slightest
movements side to side
kept me where the sun's
rays would warm me.
I needed the swaddling
of the blanket I found
at the bottom of the cupboard,
a newborn in the early
light, amused to hear
a rooster sounding his alarm
long past mine. I wanted
to sit, to rest an aching hip
I only now discovered,
but only standing planted
on the ground in the one place
I found the sun would do.

Engravings

Those sun studded summers of youth
burned into our neurons like
old photographic plates; memory
carved into the stones of the heart's lithography,
like the boulders of our Lake Huron shoreline,
placed by the gods before our teenaged feet
so we could sit and slide and dive away
those sweet, slow, never-ending days.

Those breeze soaked evenings
when our parents were elsewhere
and we turned off the lights to slow dance
in pairs, belly to belly, chest to budding breast,
protected by a naive but rock bound trust
while the artist's chemicals worked their magic,
creating images. No way to know that love
would never again be quite so innocent
or perfection this rare.

Talking Myself Down

You know that time at the circus
when the aerialists climb to the tent top—
the audience stills;
a boy swings upside down and backwards,
arms outstretched, biceps bulging, poised to catch
a girl who flies;

and a girl in spangled leotard and tights,
posed on a tiny platform high above us,
catapults herself and soars;

that time when she suspends in air—that stunning time
when no one breathes
between?

I wonder when I reach my own finale,
when flesh and spirit must take separate bows,
will the daring hurl toward new adventures,
trusting in that time between,
while I lie dizzied on a bed just feet above the floor,
clutching any hand who'll have me,
afraid to go where I have never been?

I want to leave with better grace
than all my hanging onto earth suggests.
I practice when I can on airplanes,
when turbulence and seat belt signs
become my own trapezes.

I think about the ones I love; count savings
still unused—the benefit of my untimely
end; picture well-attended funerals, console myself
by feeling missed;

I will my muscles to relax, unclench
the death grip on my seat arms;
imagine calmly flying free
like spangled girls in leotards

who dare to love the time between.

Untitled

I feel like something
is cooking in me,
gestating, percolating,
wanting to be born.
I'm afraid to tell you. Afraid
if I name it, I will
make it real and then
I'll have to live it; won't
be able to go back under
water or hide out inside
Pandora's black box.
Big stuff, beating
in my brain and belly,
more heft and lift
than I am used to.
I'm afraid to tell you.
This might be real.
And then I'll have to
live it. This.

Indian Wedding Journal 2: Howrah Station

For forty rupees, we shed the last rule
that links us to the familiar. Giant doors swing open

allowing us to drive inside the station and park
directly by the tracks. The doors shut tight behind us,

contain us in a world of simmering sepia,
sealed away from time.

Laura buys three raffia fans,
one for her mother, one for Aunt Marilyn, and one for me.

It is so hot the word has lost all meaning.
We lean against the white metal reality of our cars

to keep from melting completely into the dream.
Images come in waves.

Only the incongruous registers—
An ancient woman, reduced to child-bones

and empty breasts, emerges from the flow, extends
a leathered palm for alms and

blesses me with hands in prayer position
before her toothless smile.

Gandhi-like, a dhoti-wearing Brahmin
wears loafers on his feet instead of sandals,

A workman rolls a wooden wheel twice his size
with metal canisters tied to it.

Curious, I can't remember sound.
Women balance parcels on their heads

and move like swimmers.
A wiry man of indeterminate age carrying a tray

with white ceramic teapot and tiny paper cups,
like a host at a party, approaches and tries to sell us tea.

A well-dressed family surrounded by suitcases
sits on their bundles and calmly awaits the train;

the crowd creates a wake around them. The fading light
soaks color from the mother's sari; her children's hair

curls darkly in the heat.

Suddenly everything speeds up, becoming fuller,
rich and succulent as time-lapse photography,
swallowing the details in its rush to completion.

People appear from nowhere.
The energy begins to boil.

"The train is coming!" the bride declares.
"Get back in the cars. We will drive
down the track to find your compartment."

Time has reappeared again. I am astonished
at not figuring this out for myself. There is tension
in the bride's voice. So far she hasn't lost us,
but the crucial part of boarding comes now.
Anything might happen. We could be swept away
with this tide of people and never be seen again.

I want to tell her not to worry. We are safe
in this ocean; it is only a dream. But I am too far
under water to utter a word. The night sky darkens;
the klieg lights come on; the porters wear red,
and the one with mutton chop whiskers,
who looks like an English colonel races down the track,
beating the cars to meet us, determined to carry our bags.

The energy is moving inexorably to a climax;
where we will end up is anyone's guess.
Carried along by the passion, I no longer care.

Disconnect

Love sits on the lap of a man with iron belly
unable to get in. He has to leave her.

Despair follows the poet into her all-white bedroom
thick with silence, TV noise no longer a distraction.
She leaves the remote untouched as she.
On her bed she must feel her losses.
Weep until there's nothing left

but truth and empty space. Allow the wounds,
fear she won't find respite or, like the *Handless Maiden,*
hands that ever grow again. Despair calls her
like a visit to New York; a nice place to visit but
she doesn't want to live there, too full

of energy and texture for her now frail container,
the diversity of feeling ordinary life carpets over.
She doesn't want to emulate the edge poets,
sticking their heads in ovens
when feelings are too hard to bear.

Her strategy? A luncheon to raise money
for children who cannot read, a client to coach
for whom she's not a step ahead, a walk with a friend
who also obsesses about haircuts, a music appreciation class
she tries but can't appreciate. As last resort the bills.

Break Up Kindly

Put away all axes and meat cleavers
no matter how great your need
to sever the connection
and get yourself away.

Free yourself as though
you are sautéing small fish.
Turn them over carefully
so they won't crumble.

Don't cause trainwrecked
spirits on your tracks
to someday shame you.

Instead find courage to leave
gently as though you are a ship's
wake phosphorescent with plankton
lighting up the night.

You Can't Get Rid of an Old Love

You can't get rid of an old love
no matter how hard you try.
Erase his memory from your mind,
he's tap dancing on your bones.

He shows up in your nervous system,
in those jumpy synapses
where once he cruised, king of the road;
that unused highway you camouflaged
with weeds of disappointment.

The cover has no roots;
it blows away like dandelion fluff
when he shakes his handsome head
and wakes; a Rip Van Winkle
striding around inside you as though
he owns the place, the resident ghost,
laughing, friendly, still a con man.

You tell him, *"get the hell out."*
You're done with him. It's been years.
And anyway, he's dead now. You saw
the obituary with your own eyes.

He occupies no fixed geographic place,
which only makes it worse; now even that
puff of wind on your neck could be him;
he always was a will-o'-the-wisp,
or that odd feeling in your belly,
that handsome grove of trees—
he was a dandy, that pain
that might be tears behind your eyes.

He said he was taking his dreams
and fears away from you; you could never
know them again, but it's really elephants
all the way down.

You can't get rid of an old love.
Forget it.
It can't be done.

Dinner Companions

I was on a blind date, sitting
across a table from Experience.
He was smoking a cigar
and looking smug, having polished
off a large steak, fried potatoes and
a bottle of wine. He was contemplating
dessert, deciding between Bananas Foster
or Cherries Jubilee. He picked his teeth
with a silver toothpick taken
from his vest pocket, patted his belly
and belched. Then produced a used
linen handkerchief and dramatically
wiped a tear or two from his eye,

    "With all I've gone through," he announced,
    I owe it to myself to enjoy life as much as I can!"

To tell you the truth, he was too much
for me. He was turning me off.

But then Romance joined us
and she was worse. Dressed
like a southern belle in flounce
and flowers, with a big straw hat
on her golden curls, her violet eyes
wide with emotion, palpitations
plain to see under her heaving bodice,
she ordered Shrimp Remoulade

and raspberry tea, and then only
picked at her food. She told us she
had no appetite. She only wanted
to talk about love—new love, old love,
lost love, unrequited love.

    "There is nothing in the world to compare
    with romance," she declared.

Experience rolled his eyes at me and muttered something
under his breath. Romance sighed deeply
and gazed into the middle distance.
This conversation was giving me heartburn;
I started to feel a bit warmer toward Experience.

A tall, thin lady showed up next and asked
to join us. She introduced herself
as Patience. She was wearing a tidy
brown outfit: skirt, jacket, bag and shoes.
Her blouse was ivory and buttoned to the neck.
She promised not to take up extra room.
When the harried waitress flew by
and told her she'd get back as soon
as she could, Patience replied she was fine
to wait. I was preparing myself
for a tedious sit, when Romance seized the day
and began telling Patience about her
latest love affair; It was not going well!

Romance was distraught, but not so much
she couldn't tell a good audience
when she saw one. It was another case
where she loved him but he left her anyway,
with enough juicy tidbits to make the conversation
tolerable. I was just glad it wasn't me.

Experience continued to pick his teeth
and ponder dessert, when Goodness
made her appearance. She was dressed in
sky blue tulle and had a high voice
like Billy Burke. She told us about all the good
works she'd done and everything still
crying out for her to accomplish.
You could picture her waving a magic wand,
clicking her silver shoes together
and turning the other cheek if she didn't succeed.
This was more than I could stand
at one dinner. There was only one seat
left at the table. I told Goodness it was taken.
Experience gave me a wink, so I knew I was on
the right track. I was liking him more and more.

Sure enough, just then a round fellow
with a wide smile claimed the empty place.
He wore a red-checked shirt,
plaid trousers and a baseball cap on

backwards. He turned the chair around
and straddled it. He chuckled to himself.

"What's so funny?" Romance demanded.
"Have you been eavesdropping on our conversation?"

You could tell she was worried he might
be making fun of her.

"Nothing," he said. "My name is Laughter.
I love to laugh. Almost everything is funny to me."

He chuckled louder.
Just listening to him caused the atmosphere
around the table to start to lighten.
Experience decided to have both desserts
and began to tell the epic story
of his life. Fortunes won and fortunes lost.
Laughter chortled appreciatively.
Romance interrupted to tell the same of love.
Laughter giggled. It was beginning
to be infectious. Patience, not to be outdone,
regaled us with her story. Tempers held and
tempers lost. By then, Laughter was holding
his stomach, he was laughing so hard.
And so was I. I should have been wearing Depends.

Everyone at the table was laughing
by now. We were in such good moods

we even made room for Billy Burke,
who turned out to have a sense of humor
after all. She ordered a soda and had just
taken a sip when a new round of laughter
took her by surprise. The soda shot
out of her mouth and left a dark, wet stain
down the front of her blue tulle dress.

"So much for looking good all the time," she announced.

We were on the floor laughing. Everyone's sides hurt.

"Please," I begged, "stop. I have to catch my breath."

Laughter suggested ordering a round of hot fudge
sundaes for the table.

Patience shouted, "Hurry!"

"You can never get too much hot fudge,"
Experience avowed.

Romance retorted, "To hell with him. He either likes me plump
or he can find somebody else!"

"Ice cream isn't the best diet for starving children anyway,"
Goodness declared.

Laughter licked his spoon and smiled.

Changing Shapes

I'm not so interested these days
in shape
as I am in shapelessness
and flow.

What good does it do to change
from square to circle
or triangle to polygon or helix
when what is called for
is letting go.

I think it's best
to be like water, to be
not just the ocean, but to know
the tide and current
as supplicant and lover.

I'm not so interested
in hanging on to any shape
when the challenge
is to learn to flow;

to be the wave
that cascades, or laps,
or crashes without protest
against a hostile or a foreign
or, with luck, a gentle shore.

There is punishment in clinging.
Not God's,
but just because
it goes against the order of things.

I know that.
Yet I do it anyway.
Imitating the ocean
is presumption.

Still I haven't given up hope
of turning into
stream or river

when I remember
in the nick of time
to save myself from drowning
by refusing to shift back
into an old
discarded
shape.

How to Nurture Your Soul

Carve out big slices of time.
If you don't have a holiday carver
a kitchen knife will do.

Use your will as a wand.
You have to be ruthless.

Hollow out space like a pumpkin.
Carve windows and doorways,
make room for the senses.

Drink in every color of green—
oaks, banyans,
willows, palms,
the one that's more silver than green.

Be startled by red—
geraniums, poinsettias,
orchids, impatiens.

Touch silence.
Listen to the refrigerator hum.

Wear wind on your skin.
Breathe air in like menthol.
Read the earth in your footsteps.

Taste compassion

for those who have failings.
Start out with the fruit of yourself.

Dither, dabble, do nothing.
Inhabit your dreams.
Learn labyrinths and limbo.

Remember the soul
needs a parent.
If you don't protect it
who will?

Second Chance

Once,
standing alone at dusk,
with the Pacific
stretching beneath me,
and the mountains of Mexico
a lavender/brown haze
through my squinted eyes,
I memorized a railing.

Memorized,
as a blind person might,
with fingertips,
and hand and palm,
the delicate bits of salt
embedded
in the smoothly varnished surface,
the length, and contours,
and solidity of the wood.

Hearing the throb
of motors, and crash of prow,
cut through me
to the rushing sea.
Tasting the salt air on my lips,
minting my breath.

Giving myself over
to the railing
so that later
I could memorize
your arms.

Soul Song

A simple little melody
    was how it all began—
teasing, shy, flirtatious,
    whistled behind the teeth in snatches.
You hummed a phrase
    then stopped, before the note was finished—
just enough to catch my ear
    and tempt me to respond the chorus.

Another line from you,
    sly, beguiling, stopped just short—
then my response, a variation of the theme,
    hoping you would find the resolution.
I did not think I knew the key;
    the notes I longed to share were there but foreign.
Still I could sense the music that was you,
    and dared to dream the instrument to your musician.

An untuned cello, I—
    an untried clarinet—
frightened to offer up so poor a thing,
    yet who could bear to leave that song half sung?
I told myself *"just one more note"*;
    just one would leave me more contented.
And one and one and one and one—
    relieved you guessed my true intention.

Now you play me like a violin;
    your fingers find the secret harmonies;
lips—tongue—teeth—breath—
    exposing notes so pure at first they hurt.
Your voice sets me; a metronome.
    While you compose exotic lyric
blending truth to heart and bone
    until I beg to join the orchestration.

A bawdy, brassy trumpet, I—
    a balalaika, sensuous, wooing—
an aria, a lullaby—
    The Hallelujah Chorus rising.
I did not think that I could sing
    and yet I longed to write a score;
plucking honeyed chords
    from sunlight, grasses moist,
warmed passageways of earth and sky—
    We are the music of our own creation.

Memorable Strangers

You could not call them intimates,
these nine daughters of Zeus and Mnemosyne,
or even friends;
they are too unreliable for that.
They are always strangers,
coming and going at will,
at odd hours, when the spirit moves them,
clamming up just when you think you've gotten to know them,
abandoning you for someone they like better,
indifferent to your angst, your need.

Yet all the more memorable for that;
the way they show up when least expected
after you've spent hours turning out not art, but compost,
the polite word for garbage, dung, crap, manure.
The sweet way suddenly the puzzle pieces fit together;
the hour the words begin to write themselves;
the day the music sings.
You know it's not you doing this;
at least not you alone. How could it be?
Some Muse has finally pitied you
and deigned to send you grace.
How can you ever forget something like that?

Maybe it's because they were raised as goddesses;
they are used to calling the shots.
They like keeping you guessing;
they adore center stage.

Who wouldn't like to be worshipped,
applauded, and loved?
Calliope carrying her writing tablet,
Melpomene and Thalia wearing masks;
Polyhymnia looking pensive;
Erato with her lyre and crown of roses;
Clio holding her scroll and books, Euterpe with her flute;
Terpsichore dancing; Urania complete with staff and globe.

For Sara
–Who Always Believed

We all saw the resemblance;
it was that remarkable—
the auburn colored hair
in a bowl-shaped cut,
the rounded body,
that same lack of self-consciousness,
the artist's way her eyes watched us
as though we were the subject
instead of her.

It was years before we dared
to tell her—her double
at the Detroit Zoo—
afraid we'd hurt her feelings.
We forgot her sense of humor,
her attraction to the unique
and bizarre:

Edvard Munch. Lennie Bruce.
Willem de Kooning. *"Why
didn't you take a picture?"*
she wanted to know,
so she could see
with her own eyes.

After all, wasn't it she, forty
and fascinated, who plunged down
Marcel Duchamp's staircase
and emerged at the bottom,
somehow, intact and energized,
master's thesis in tow?

So an orangutan look-alike
only amused her; another reminder,
like the nail polish she found
that summer in India, of how,
on the best days, life's audacity
imagines itself into art.

Joseph Cornell. Lucas
Samaras. *Mauve Enigma.*

A Question of Time

I wanted to write about Grace
whose surgery was so rare
even her doctors didn't know
what to expect in her healing;
who found answers from a source,
unexpected—three strangers in three
separate places whose haircuts
she greatly admired. She hated the scar
on the back of her head, the abysmal ways
it confounded her hair. It turned out
that hairdresser's husband had the same surgery
and had mended, to Grace's relief,
perfectly well. But I don't have time to do justice
to such a good story about the synchronicities
of life and why Grace was lucky
and got what she needed.

Or I could tell you about
Grandfather Louis
who died by his own hand
when my mother, the youngest of six,
was a baby—though the secret
didn't come out until long after I was grown.
Why such drastic action? What shame or despair
drove him to do this? My mother seemed unmoved
by the revelation. She said it was hard to miss
what you never had. Still, he took up a lot of room
in the family—the Black Hole that was my grandfather.

It would be worth pondering the questions his life,
and especially his death, might have answered.
I've often wanted to try. But I would have to
make him up, and right now I don't have time
to get into a mystery like that.

So I will relate the story of
my granddaughter Lauren's
missing computer game piece,
the size of a postage stamp, and how relieved
I was that this time I could put it in an ordinary
envelope if it turned up—though I doubted it would—
instead of having to trek to the post office,
since someone was always forgetting something
when they visited and asking me to mail it
back to them—which I confess
was annoying. But this time, at the last minute,
my daughter-in-law found it wedged
under the base of the butler's rack
in the den. It was so thin, it's likely
it would never have been found
until after we were dead, which tells you
it's good to know what you're looking for—
and it's important who does the looking—
because sometimes all the pieces
do come together and there is time
to tell the whole story, even though
it's a little one.

Hurricane Shutters

Every day for two weeks
the young men glide in and out.
They carry steel shutters,
drills, saws, ladders, cables,
Gatorade; testosterone
in every pocket. This is something
I've been dreading. The disruption,
lack of privacy, the mess.
But they surprise me. They try
not to invade more than they have to.
They are polite.

The one with dreadlocked mustache
and purple eyes plans a pirate wedding and wants
to look the part. He dresses in cutoff jeans,
tattoos, large gold cross; his manners
like Sunday go-to-meeting clothes.
He shows me how his dreadlocks are anchored
by fishing weights, the way he seems
weighted to the earth.

Another sports carpenter skirts like
a kilt, a midnight
black beard, his legs fine—
muscled as any nobleman's.
He plays the beams like bagpipes.
He likes to chat, but leaves to visit

in-laws near Chicago before the job
is done. His story is unfinished.

One has a glass eye, no kids,
so weekends are relaxing,
especially when his wife works.
He tells me he loves the feeling he gets
on tall buildings, the peace that comes
from being alone, suspended in air
as though he's flying. "The money is good
for work like that," he says.

I want to know how he lost his eye,
but think it rude to ask.
I think of my two sons
flying everywhere,
carrying M.B.A.'s, smartphones,
laptops, charts, statistics
briefcases, gym memberships
ties, and tension,
so there is never any real time off,
and wonder if their lives are better?

I worry when I hear the schedule of
the one prone to skin rashes who never seems to sleep,
the ragged cuticles on the fingers of the one
who hardly gets to see his children,
and when he's home, he's working still,

while the dreadlocks on the mustachioed workman
suggest freedom, and the carpenter skirted fellow
announce panache.

But then they aren't my children. I only see
gleaming muscles, smell man smells, offer
water, enjoy the way they call me "ma'am."
I don't have to own the tattoos;
I just get to visit their world for a while,
wonder what it's like to inhabit their
work boots, imbibe their competence and strength,

hear about their families,
imagine the ride when they take their weekend kids
on go-carts; hear what feeds, and hurts
and entertains them, and wonder
whose lives are better?

Managing a Planet

I can't be the only person
to have had this epiphany—

how the circus is not an escape at all,
but instead, a mirror;

how the ringmasters in flashy suits
are just actors with big voices
who pretend to know how to run these shows;

how the clowns with painted tears
who trip over everything
and chase around in circles
have a familiar ring;

how the animals might roar for a reason;
how they could escape their bars
and trample us, shake off their riders
and stampede;

how the ladies in leotards
who fly through air above us
might not be caught one day
by the men with bulging biceps
hanging upside down
and backwards;

how all of us are doing
this high wire act
without a net
together;

how all of us could fall;

how we might only be able
to swallow so many swords, juggle
so many balls, jump through
so many hoops of fire

before the greatest show
on Earth
runs out of encores;

how even at age four I felt disquiet
at the circus;

how the cotton candy
has been a bribe to distract us—

how the tickets don't come with
money back guarantees.

Silence

Listen. Do you hear it?
Hands signing space.
Ears turned into tuning forks.
That barest of hums.

Can I write so you hear it?

That slight high-pitched crackle.
Autographs of air recorded
on cheeks. Harmonies of stories
wandering the wind.

Listen. Shhhh. Listen.

Listen with me to silence.
I crave it. Then I will be quiet
and listen to you.

august
(for Jackie and the others)

We fall in love
with
rocky
earth
stones   magnified
by water clear and   moving;

Greedy women/children
pockets
filled
to burst,
gather hearty portions;

stars and messages
we dare to ask for;

Sand
between
our
toes.

Tantric Breathing

Paddling back to camp from the small island
after the heat stroke and the disappointment
had subsided; the others gone on to see
the bald eagle's nest a portage and lake away,
we came upon a deer standing alone
in the marsh grass along the near shore,
so close we could almost touch it—
a magician's gift in the yellow light of
afternoon. We froze on an in-breath,
raised our paddles slowly—
slowly
and with exquisite care
from the clear green water,
as though the air itself was fragile,
and any sound or movement
would tear us from the moment.
The deer remained unmoving, gazing at us
in what seemed equal fascination—
wilderness creatures,
breathing together
in rhythm.

Sometimes It All Dies

Those creative juices—like the red grapes
in the glass dish on the top shelf
of the refrigerator, now wrinkled
as raisins. No longer fit to be consumed,
yet no one wants to throw them out,
as though some miracle of resurrection
might still be possible.
Or maybe someone will come along
starved enough to want to eat them.

How does this happen—weeks of harvest,
poems and stories sweet on every vine and bush—
then gone one day, a wasteland?
As though words have lost their strength
to grow; the passion in the writer's soil
turned barren.

What is needed here? Plow through, sow seeds
so poor and piteous that only weeds would likely flower;
hope anyway for rain and blooming, or heed the wisdom
of the farmer who knows when time has come
for land to rest, lie fallow?
And oh, to know the difference.

Belated Gifts

—after Mary Oliver and Billy Collins

I long to write a poem
like Mary Oliver or Billy Collins,
to find a sensibility
that puts me into their exalted league.

But what did I do to deserve this?
Did I once lie on my back and study the sky
for wild geese returning to announce
how I fit into the family of things?

Did I come back from a walk in the woods
to a wooden desk lit by a window
and dash off a clever elegy
to a poem in my head, but forgotten?

No, the only journey I took this day
was to *Sam's Club* where I communed
with the wares; brought home
a mammoth box of trash bags,

a giant container of dishwasher tabs,
a vast three-berry pie,
and a pair of plump rotisserie chickens
which I proceeded to cut up

and doctor with barbecue sauce
before freezing
so I can whip them out later
to present as my own.

Poetry Where You Least Expect It

Who would have thought a broken
left metatarsal bone could inspire poetry?
Not I, clumping around all week
in this heavy black boot
replete with stays and Velcro straps
like Jack's noisy giant who lived at the top
of that unstable beanstalk—
though I only crashed down a frivolous shoe.

Then the doctor today,
as he put on the second week's cast,
described the new bone cells
as flying in V formation to mend the fracture;
drew pictures in the air with healing/artist fingers,
"Six on each side," he said, *"like birds…"*
He stopped in midsentence;
shook his head at the wonder of it.
"It's funny how nature works," he said.

Observations to My Grandsons Upon Their College Graduations

There is no one-size-fits-all
T-shirt of a poem, or rightful calling.
Neither Burberry, Old Navy or baseball shops
stock them, which sometimes seems a shame,
since some of the most promising seeds
fail to germinate. A poem, an essay,
extra innings or the right job
aren't always easy to find.

Others are like coffee grounds.
Keep working toward what you want,
even if it seems backwards, sideways or boring.
Leave them alone to percolate while you gain experience.
Eventually they pour into your waiting cup
full of flavor and bouquet, every drop a satisfaction.

Some of the best are born
entirely in your body.
You just have to get quiet; listen
to the shorthand and transcribe.
Those are the ones with breath and bones,
your blood the lucky recipient.

Sometimes you can have a mood down cold,
with an objective correlative
worthy to wear it.
Still, it can take years of trying on

until the poem finds its footing
in iambic pentameter and you can form a sonnet,
hit the winning run or write the software
to your calling.

Be patient with straight paths and detours.
Borrow Billy Collin's flashlight, his ski mask,
and window. Explore Auden. Imitate Grace Hopper,
Edison, Emily Dickinson, Dennis Eckersley,
Dustin Pedroia, Lincoln, Grant, and Shakespeare.
Be eclectic, egalitarian, excited.
Be grateful to mentors. Relax.
You're building a life, not waving a wand.

Keep your eyes peeled, dreams alive and nose to the grindstone.
Lie on your belly in the grass of your mind; open yourself
to surprises. Keep trying. (I know! Sigh!
Soon you'll be tasked to pay dues. Worse yet, taxes!
But refuse to suffer over suffering. Instead
call it privilege and growth.) You can't always know
when right work, the triple play, or a poem will arise. Or where.

One of my favorite poems came from a broken ankle,
an essay from a time when Gramp was troubled, my calling
from a job never imagined, the opportunity from a boss I detested.

So, Max and Ethan, fellow writers, my grandsons
whom I love more than these words can say,
I cheer each of you on as you take
your next steps into the world of adulthood.

From the heart,

Granny

Indian Wedding Journal 3: On the Way to Howrah Station

Leaving the bride's parents' apartment
for the last time,
the three white Ambassadors loaded—
backpacks, cases, carry-ons,
water bottles, medicinal remedies,
and food—

eleven of us, and three drivers
cavalcade through the crushed streets of Calcutta,
as though in state, to the railway station;

past the round, ivory-hued marble monument
to Queen Victoria we never saw up close,
the monsoon-washed green
of the race track grounds,

red brick government buildings trimmed like wedding cakes,
the multi-colored shrines of the homeless,
patinaed shacks of the poor.

We push our way through the usual cacophony
of horns honking, people crossing, trucks rumbling, children calling,
tires screeching, rickshaws running, women carrying, cows meandering,
men gambling, buses careening, people buying, selling, cooking, eating,
barbering, begging, standing, waiting, sewing, fixing, sitting, sleeping,
scooters cycling, bullocks lumbering, cars passing, exhausts belching…
with barely a whisper of space between us.

Then, just before our drive across the Hooghly River,
a woman living in a cage
hidden away under Howrah Bridge
turns suddenly and challenges my gaze.

Only this time,
because we are leaving,
with the wedding finished,
and other agendas accomplished,

encased within the illusion
of our tough Ambassador cars,
I see Calcutta as a place
I want to remember;
now that I've grown bigger eyes.

To Wild Woman

—In honor of Clarissa Pinkola Estes, Natalie Goldberg, and all who
help the hands grow back.

Cast out of the Kingdom
to find the second half of life,
lost and confused, the light
covered over by clouds,
wanting a tree to lean on,
but none in sight
is big enough to hold her,

too tired to wander further,
she lies down on the forest floor
to rest. Dead branches, dirt,
and moss—the rich scent fills her
nostrils. Decaying leaves beneath,
she joins the compost. Tendrils
of things still living curl
around her. Rains nourish.

Small shoots emerge from spaces
between her toes and fingers,
belly button, underarms, along
her groin and scalp. She begins
to take root.

Sun warms. Leaves cover. Snow
protects. Spring again. Then
summer. Fall. Winter comes.
The cycle is repeated. Growing
into earth takes time.
Each spring the roots go deeper.

Finally,
green buds appear on tongue
and eyelids, edges of her
inner ear. Whisper to her
of the promise. Witness
that it will be kept.

In her treeness, she will flower.
This time there is no doubt.
Soil is proper. Seed willing.
Seasons honored. Roots are home.

What Remains

It takes so long
to peel skin from your orange
self you could be dried up
dead before you dare disorder,
laugh yourself sticky, drink
the sky, become cerulean blue.

Better do it now,
devour the peach before
it's shriveled. Let juice
and bits of yellow pulp
define you, snail along
your tongue, create tributaries
down your chin, then beach
like tiny landing crafts in the soft
crevices of your neck.

Find compassion for critics,
the ones who leave and those
alive in you who fear such messy
appetites. Wear a bright orange
fool's cap on your head to keep
the heat from leaving when
you have to cry, its tasseled bells
remind there is no need to find
false skins for cover. The unpeeled
flesh is where your juice remains.

ACKNOWLEDGEMENTS

With thanks to the editors, the following poems from this collection have appeared, sometimes in a slightly different form or under a different title in these publications:

"First Thaw," *Voices Israel Anthology 2019.*

"Tantric Breathing," 2019 Flagler County Art League's Poetry Competition winning poems (web).

"Break Up Kindly," *We'Moon Datebook 2018.*

"What Remains" and "Break Up Kindly," *Voices Israel Annual Anthology 2018.*

"You Can't Get Rid of an Old Love," *Voices Israel Annual Anthology 2015.*

"Bone on Bone," *Voices Israel Annual Anthology 2015.*

"When They Were Born," previously published under the title "When He Was Born," *Voices Israel Anthology 2019,* and the title "When You Were Born," *Cyclamens and Swords,* August 2015.

"How to Nurture Your Soul," *Today's Caregiver 2014 Conference Guide.*

"Managing a Planet," *We'Moon Datebook 2014.*

"Gender Negotiation," Fellowship in Prayer, Winter 2012.

"Tulip Bulbs," *Living with Loss Magazine*, Spring 2012 Issue.

"Of Physicists and Elegies," *23rd Annual Iowa Summer Writing Festival Anthology*, The University of Iowa, July 2009; and *The Healing Muse*, Issue 10, October 13, 2010.

"A Small Bird," *Blank Canvas Pocket-Edition: Shalla Magazine* (Volume 1), Jan. 2010; *Other Voices International Project*, Vol. 41, April 2009; *Shalla Magazine*, March 2009; and *Borderlines Vol. II Literary Anthology*, a publication of the University of Portsmouth, United Kingdom, Summer 2008.

"On the Ganges" Dyer-Ives Foundation Poetry Prize Book (*Voices*) and *Other Voices International Project*, Vol. 41, April 2009.

"Recipe" Dyer-Ives Foundation Poetry Prize Book, (*Voices*), and *Other Voices International Project*, Vol. 41, April 2009.

"Reflection," *Other Voices International Project*, Vol. 41, April 2009.

"Gemini in a Mood," *We'Moon 99*.

"At Taos Pueblo," "august," and "Witch Dead, Spell Broken, Awakened Princess Connects with Pea," *Fallen Angels, 1992, Taos, New Mexico, Natalie Goldberg, Kate Green Workshop Anthology*.

"Second Chance," previously published in a slightly different format under the title "Once I Memorized a Railing," Dyer-Ives Foundation Poetry Prize Book (*Voices*).

"April Sonnet," ORBIT and the Olivet Prize Book.

"This is the Year the Dead Come Marching," *SNReview*, Autumn 2008, Volume 10 Issue 3; and

Other Voices International Project, Vol. 41, April 2009.

"Sometimes It All Dies," *SNReview*, Autumn 2008, Volume 10 Issue 3.

"Reflection," *SNReview*, Autumn 2008, Volume 10 Issue 3.

More gratitude than I can find words to express to my family, living and dead, who are my heart, my home, my inspiration, my roots— and to Stu, who with remarkable patience stands beside me. Deep appreciation to the many friends, colleagues and teachers who have mentored and supported me; and to Barbara Delage of Springboard Literary without whose caring and expertise this book would still be sitting in my computer.

ABOUT THE AUTHOR

Since publication in *McCall's Magazine* and *The Wall Street Journal* in the 1960s, Linda Albert's poems and essays have appeared internationally in numerous magazines, journals and anthologies. She is a recipient of the Atlanta Review Merit Award, an Olivet College Sonnet Competition prize and three Dyer-Ives Foundation Poetry Prizes.

A spiritual preview at age 29 inspired Linda to a quest for personal wholeness and ways to give back to others. Acting, directing, reading, research, real estate sales, and workshops ranging from writing, shamanism, intuition training, spiritual direction and mind development to graduate university classes ultimately led her to teaching.

She became master certified in Neuro-Linguistics, a unique approach to communication offering practical applications to her work, life, and writing. A listening trainer at a communications consulting firm, she later founded her own coaching practice, and also taught at education centers in Michigan and Florida.

The psychology of Carl Jung with its emphasis on *individuation*—a second half of life directive to live as courageously and authentically the largest lives of which we are capable—aligned with Linda's inner calling. After her husband's death, she studied at the Assisi Institute, the International Center for the Study of Archetypal Patterns earning certifications in Archetypal Pattern Analysis and Dream Translation, focusing most recently on conscious and creative aging.

A Detroit native and mother of four, Linda lives full-time in Sarasota, Florida. Visit her online at www.lindaalbert.net.

Made in the USA
Middletown, DE
19 January 2021